The Best Of *The Mailbox*®
Bulletin Boards
Primary Edition

Y0-BBY-540

Our favorite bulletin boards from the
issues of the Primary edition of *The Mailbox*® magazine

Editor In Chief:
Margaret Michel

Product Director:
Kathy Wolf

Editors:
Diane Badden
Cynthia Holcolmb
Laurel Robinson

Artists:
Jennifer Tipton Bennett
Cathy Spangler Bruce
Donna Teal

Cover Design:
Jim Counts

Visit our Web site at www.themailbox.com.

About This Book

The Best Of The Mailbox® *Bulletin Boards Primary* is a collection of the best bulletin boards published in the Primary editions of *The Mailbox®* from 1988 to 1994. It was designed to provide an extensive collection of motivating, teacher-created, easy-to-make bulletin boards for today's busy teacher. All of the displays involve student participation and make attractive classroom displays.

The book is divided into four sections: Fall, Winter, Spring, and Anytime. There are 90 illustrations of bulletin boards which include complete instructions as well as reproducible patterns.

www.themailbox.com

©1996 by THE EDUCATION CENTER, INC.
All rights reserved.
ISBN# 1-56234-147-2

Manufactured in the United States
10 9 8 7 6 5

Table Of Contents

FALL

Fall Bulletin Boards ....

Make way for these little ducklings on your back-to-school bulletin board! Duplicate the pattern on page 55 onto yellow construction paper; then label and cut out one pattern for each child. Complete an enlarged pattern for yourself. Mount cutouts as shown. Your students will go "quackers" over this one!

Mary Dinneen—Gr. 2, Mountain View School, Bristol, CT

Here's a team that can outshine any of its competition! On white construction paper, duplicate student copies of the pattern on page 56. Have each student cut out a pattern, then decorate the resulting cutout to resemble himself. Provide an assortment of arts-and-crafts supplies including crayons, yarn, buttons, scraps of fabric, construction paper, and wallpaper. Mount the cutouts, a student-generated list of "team rules," and the title as shown. Go team! Go!

Kathy Lezotte-Zuck—Gr. 1, Ladysmith Elementary School, Ladysmith, WI

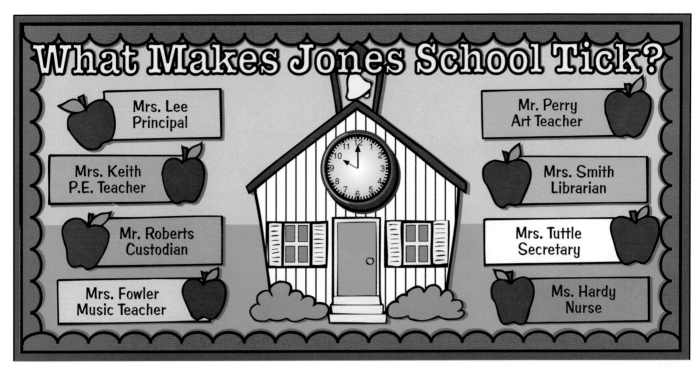

Create this timely display in a matter of minutes! Mount a large schoolhouse cutout (pattern on page 57); then suspend a battery-operated clock from a pushpin inserted into the cutout. Attach construction-paper rectangles bearing the names and occupations of selected school staff members. Add apple cutouts (pattern on page 57), the title, and a border to complete the display. Ticktock! Ticktock!

Amy Griffin, Tarboro, NC

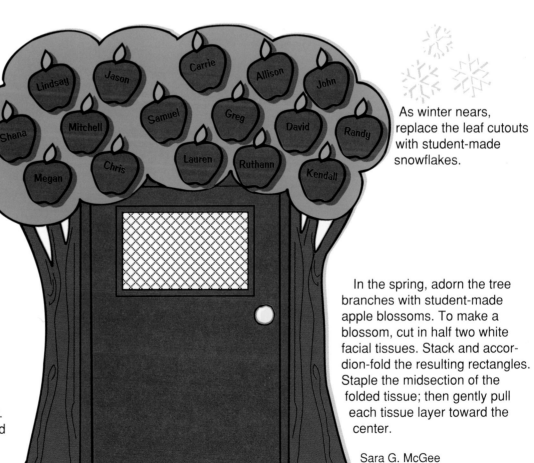

Here's a "tree-mendous" year-round display! Cut and mount (around a door frame) lengths of brown paper to resemble a tree trunk and branches. For a back-to-school display, attach a large, green treetop cutout atop the upper tree branches. Attach student-made apple cutouts to the treetop.

As winter nears, replace the leaf cutouts with student-made snowflakes.

In the spring, adorn the tree branches with student-made apple blossoms. To make a blossom, cut in half two white facial tissues. Stack and accordion-fold the resulting rectangles. Staple the midsection of the folded tissue; then gently pull each tissue layer toward the center.

For a fall display, have students cut leaf shapes from red, orange, and yellow paper. Remove the treetop cutout and attach the leaf cutouts to the underlying tree branches.

Sara G. McGee
Bel Air Elementary
Evans, GA

"Bear-y" Special Students

Begin the year in a "bear-y" special way with this first-day activity. Duplicate a bear pattern (page 58) on brown construction paper for each student. Instruct students to cut out and "dress" their bear patterns to look exactly as they did when they arrived at school that morning. (Provide construction paper of assorted colors, scissors, crayons, and glue for the students to use.) Attach the completed cutouts to a bulletin board titled "'Bear-y' Special Students."

Dianne Krieser—Gr. 3, Hamlow Elementary School, Waverly, NE

Let's Work Together

Invite your students to "lend a hand" in planning possible lessons for the new school year. Each student traces his hand outline onto a sheet of construction paper, cuts out the outline, then (inside his cutout) writes his name and a sentence telling one thing he would like to learn. Display the completed cutouts in a wreath shape. Make this a year-round bulletin board by attaching foil stars to the cutouts when the ideas written on them have been taught.

Marilyn Borden—Gr. 3
Castleton Elementary School
Bomoseen, VT

Create an appetite for learning with this versatile display. Mount the character (pattern on page 59) and title. Have each student trim a construction-paper square into a cookie shape, then personalize and decorate the resulting cutout. On writing paper, have students write their goals for the school year. Mount the cookies and papers as shown. Periodically have students evaluate and rewrite their goals. Or invite youngsters to showcase their best work throughout the year at the display. Now you're cookin'!

Diane Afferton—Gr. 3, Morrisville, PA

This one-of-a-kind display is sure to be a hands-down favorite! Post the title on a bulletin board covered with colorful butcher paper. On the first day of school, have each student place his hand, palm down, in poster paint and press it on the butcher paper to create a handprint. Have students add their signatures near their prints. Now that's a handy-dandy display!

9

Start the year off right with this roundup of tips! Mount the tips, character (pattern on page 60), and length of rope as shown. For a star-studded border, have each youngster personalize a construction-paper badge cutout. Then corral your buckaroos and challenge them to try their hands at working together. In no time at all, your cowpokes will be kicking up their heels in unison!

Diane Roberts—Gr. 2, Little Egg Harbor Primary School, Lanoka Harbor, NJ

Here's an easy-to-make helper display that you can use all year long! Post the title and desired job descriptions on a bulletin board covered with newspaper from the classified section. Have each student cut out, personalize, and decorate a construction-paper pattern (page 56) to resemble himself. Pin one cutout below each job description. Store the remaining cutouts nearby. Each week assign new jobs using an established method of rotation.

Margo Stocker—Gr. 3, Isbister School, Plymouth, MI

Proclaim to all who enter that inside your classroom "The Sky's The Limit!" In the hallway above your classroom door, mount a painted rainbow cutout and two cloud shapes cut from fiberfill. Have students personalize, decorate, and cut out duplicated airplane patterns (pattern on page 61). Display completed cutouts and title as shown. Your flight pattern for a super year has been confirmed!

Nancy Dunn and Darlene Milholen
Silk Hope Elementary
Siler City, NC

Celebrate the beginning of a great year with this colorful lift-off! Decorate one of two matching balloon cutouts (page 62). Place crumpled tissue paper between the cutouts; then staple and mount on the bulletin board. Bend and attach strips of ribbed bulletin-board border to form the balloon basket, completing the three-dimensional display. Students label and color circle cutouts for balloons. Mount each student's cutout above a brown construction-paper square bearing his photo. Use pipe cleaners or yarn lengths to connect the balloon and basket cutouts. Up, up, and away!

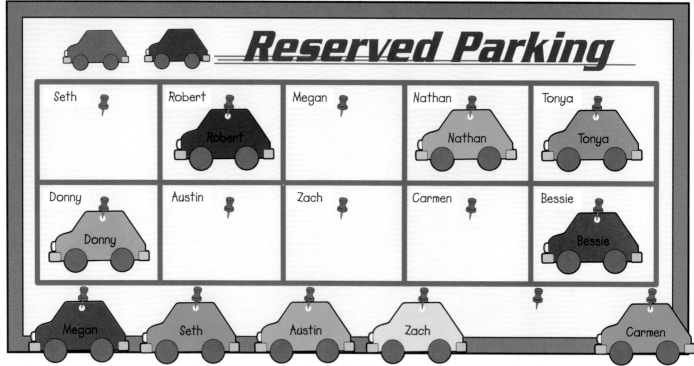

Parking won't be a problem at this attendance bulletin board. Use yarn lengths to section off a bulletin board. Place a pushpin and a student nametag in each section. Students label, decorate, and cut out duplicated copies of the car pattern on page 63. Or students can mount magazine cutouts atop precut and labeled tagboard pieces. Laminate and punch a hole in each cutout. Students park their cutouts in the reserved spaces each day as they arrive. As they leave for the day, students move their cutouts to pushpins located along the lower edge of the board.

Marilyn Borden—Gr. 3, Castleton Elementary School, Bomoseen, VT

Who would guess that raking leaves could be so much fun? Duplicate and cut out several construction-paper leaves (pattern on page 63). Display a few leaf cutouts in piles, then attach a press-on pocket atop each pile as shown. Laminate and punch holes in the remaining leaf cutouts. Program these cutouts with math facts and the press-on pockets with corresponding answers. Hang the cutouts from pins inserted in a large tree cutout. Students place the leaf cutouts in appropriate pockets. Reprogram the leaf cutouts and press-on pockets for a variety of skills throughout the fall season.

Steps In Discovery

May

March

Jan.

Nov.

Sept.

June

April

Feb.

Dec.

Oct.

Joel

Keri

Take these steps toward a year full of learning and discovery. Using brown grocery bags, create a three-dimensional, ten-rung ladder like the one shown. Then, beginning at the bottom rung, label one rung for each month of the school year. Mount an assortment of student projects throughout the year. Easy does it!

Danielle R. Nanna—Gr. 2
Wilchester Elementary
Houston, TX

Sail On, Columbus

Micky
My big dream is to find homes for the homeless.

Sarah
My big dream is to walk on the moon.

Lee
My big dream is to become a world-famous cook.

Artemon
My big dream is to win an Olympic gold medal.

Jason
My big dream is to write children's books.

Beth
My big dream is to become the first woman president.

Candice
My big dream is to find a cure for AIDS.

Ashley
My big dream is to become a movie star.

This seaworthy display encourages youngsters to follow their dreams. Using the instructions on page 64 and 65, have each youngster design a ship and write his biggest dream on a cloud cutout. Next have each youngster cut a bottle shape from dark blue paper, mount his ship atop the resulting cutout, and cover the project with a length of clear plastic wrap. Mount each youngster's ship project and cloud cutout. What a fleet!

Carla T. Jurukov—Gr. 3, John Muir School, Glendale, CA

13

This motivational bulletin board is also a great holiday decoration. Keep an ongoing display of outstanding student work for the month of October. (See patterns on page 66.)

Debbie Wiggins, Myrtle Beach Elementary, Myrtle Beach, SC

Reap a crop of outstanding student work with this eye-catching display. Mount several pumpkin cutouts and a scarecrow cutout (pattern on page 67). Attach title letters cut from burlap material. If desired, add lengths of raffia (to imitate straw) and scraps of burlap and felt materials as scarecrow decorations. Have students prepare realistic leaf cutouts to complete the display.

Shelly Johnson, Fairfield, MT

Scare up some Halloween fun with this "spook-tacular" display! Laminate five large ghost cutouts similar to the ones shown. Using a wipe-off marker, program each cutout with a Halloween riddle. Challenge youngsters to write the answers to the riddles on answer sheets. A few days later, reveal the correct riddle answers and award Halloween stickers as desired. Then wipe away the programming, reprogram the cutouts, and repeat the procedure. (See page 68 for riddle answers and pattern.)

Cindy Fischer—Gr. 1, St. Mary's School, Bismarck, ND

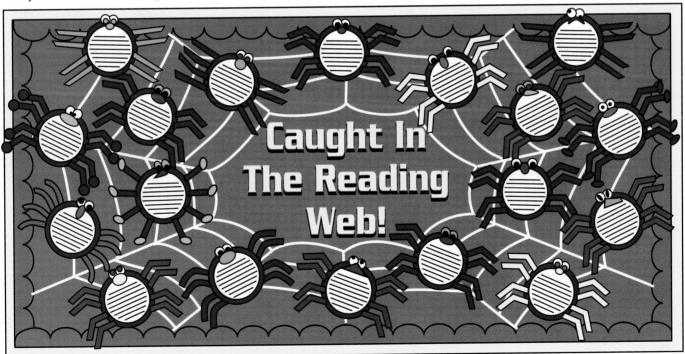

Spin a web of reading motivation with this "spider-ific" display. Mount the title and attach a yarn web. Duplicate a supply of circular book-report forms. A student completes one of these reports for each book that he reads. He mounts his report onto black construction-paper cutouts of the spider on page 69. Attach the completed projects to the web.

adapted from an idea by Ann E. Fausnight, Canton, OH

Invite youngsters to showcase their best work at this nutty display. Mount the character (pattern on page 70) and title. On light brown construction paper, duplicate a student supply of acorn paper toppers using the patterns on page 71. Have each student personalize, decorate, and cut out a paper topper. Then have each student choose a sample of her best work. Display the work samples and paper toppers as shown. Periodically ask students to replace their displayed work with more current samples. That's it in a nutshell!

Mary Dinneen—Gr. 2, Mountain View School, Bristol, CT

Stir up a batch of thankful thoughts for this year's Thanksgiving celebration. On a duplicated recipe card (pattern on page 74), have each student list six necessary ingredients for a thankful Thanksgiving. Then have him write instructions explaining how these ingredients can be used to create a thankful celebration. Next have each student mount his completed card on a 6" x 9" sheet of construction paper, then trim and personalize his project as desired. Enlarge, color, and duplicate the turkey pattern on page 72. Gobble, gobble!

Use a little "footwork" to create this colorful gobbler! To make the body, have students attach twisted tissue-paper squares to cover a large, circular tagboard cutout. Atop the body attach a construction-paper cutout in the shape of a turkey head (pattern page 73). Next add construction-paper feet, eyes, a beak and a red tissue-paper wattle. For turkey feathers, students trace and cut out their footprints from sheets of brightly colored paper. Now that's a good-lookin' gobbler!

Vivian Campbell—Gr. 1
Grandview School
Piscataway, NJ

Reap a bountiful crop of thankful thoughts this November. Ask students to cut pumpkin shapes from orange bulletin-board paper and write their thankful thoughts on the resulting cutouts. Then have students cut out, personalize, and attach green paper stems to their projects. Mount the title, cutouts, and completed pumpkin projects as shown. Use the pumpkin and pilgrim patterns on page 75 and 76. Let the harvest begin!

"Tree-mendously" Thankful Thoughts!

Branch out with this three-dimensional student-made display! To make the branches, have each youngster cut a large grocery bag down one side and then cut to detach the bottom of the bag. Next have each student flatten and roll the resulting paper to create a tree branch. Using the patterns on page 77, duplicate a supply of fall-colored leaves. Have students cut out and label each leaf with a thankful thought. Mount the branches and leaves in a desired fashion.

Janet Chadwick—Gr. 2, Monte Vista Elementary, La Crescenta, CA

Gracias Por...

Ropa

Comida

Mi Familia

Amigos

Reinforce your youngsters' Spanish or have fun introducing new Spanish words and phrases with this seasonal display. Enlarge, color, and cut out the turkey patterns on page 73. With your youngsters' input, determine four or more desired categories. Then have each youngster complete an illustration for the category of his choice. Before attaching the students' projects to the display, have each youngster share his illustration and name its category. Magnífico!

Jean Garza—Gr. 2, Country Club School, Farmington, NM

WINTER

GLUE

Winter Bulletin Boards..............................

Hanukkah greetings abound from this shimmery display. Each Star of David is made from six Popsicle® sticks. Using a cotton swab, spread a thin coat of glue over each stick; then sprinkle with gold glitter. Form two triangles of three sticks each and glue in place. Finally arrange triangles into the Star of David shape and glue. Mount each student's project and title the display "Happy Hanukkah!"

Students adorn this Christmas tree cutout with colorful decorations as they complete outstanding work. Each time a student earns a sticker for outstanding work, allow him to place his reward on the tree. This attractive display greatly motivates "star" students to complete top-notch work throughout the holiday season!

Jean Shedrick and Donna Beech, Assawompset School, Lakeville, MA

This holiday season set your room aglow with outstanding student work. Mount a large candle cutout, the title, and one 9" x 12" sheet of construction paper per student. Have each youngster initial and cut out a construction-paper flame; then staple the flames above the sheets of construction paper. Have each student select a sample of his best work. Attach the work samples to the candles as shown. Ask students to replace their work samples weekly.

Margaret Leyen—Gr. 2, Pineview Elementary, Iowa Falls, IA

Gift-wrapping paper featuring snow-covered houses gives this student-made holiday scene its unusual character. Cut wrapping paper for borders. Using colors similar to those in the wrapping paper, have each student make his own house from bulletin-board paper or construction paper. Have students decorate the houses using markers, and glue on cotton balls for snow. Students cut out foil trees and stars to complete the effect.

Carole Joros and Barb Brewer, Arcola Elementary School, Arcola, IN

You'll receive a jolly response when you display these student-made projects. To make a reindeer, bend a clothes hanger into a diamond shape. Stretch one leg of a pair of pantyhose over the hanger, pulling it toward the hook. At the base of the hook, secure the hose with a piece of yarn or string. Cut antlers, eyes, a nose, and other desired decorations from construction paper. Glue the cutouts to the hose. Mount the completed projects and the title as shown.

Vivian Campbell—Gr. 2, Knollwood School, Piscataway, NJ

Frosty the Snowman would definitely have eyes for this seasonal display! Using the instructions and pattern on page 78, students create versions of Frosty's magical hat. To extend the activity, have each student trace and cut out a matching hat shape from lined paper and write a story about his magical adventure while wearing "that old silk hat." Display completed hats and stories (one atop the other) as shown.

Patricia Hipp—Gr. 1, Grandview School, Piscataway, NJ

Dress Frosty in fashion. After creating desired snowfolk cutouts, have students color half-sheets of graph paper by alternating two or more colors of crayons or markers. On the backs of these papers, have students draw and cut out mittens, buttons, scarves, and hats. Finally have students attach the colorful clothing to their snowfolk. Mount the completed projects on a display like the one shown.

Leslie A. Hoffman—Gr. 1, St. Michael's Elementary, Hastings, NE

Everyone wants a chance to be the coolest in the class. Make this motivational bulletin board to encourage good behavior. Cover the board with blue background paper, and add a border of white paper cut to resemble icicles. Duplicate the bear pattern on page 79 for each child to color and cut out. Label bears with students' names. Mount bears on ice cubes cut from white paper.

Michelle Martin, Hamilton School, Macon, GA

Ring in the new year with this star-studded display. To create the skyline, divide students into small groups and have each group sketch and cut out the silhouette of a skyscraper from black paper. Staple the cutouts to the lower edge of a bulletin board. Next have each youngster cut out and personalize a construction-paper star. Mount the stars and title as shown. When the display is completed, ask each student to make a wish (upon his star) for the new year.

Diane McMichael, Jefferson Elementary, Vincent, OH

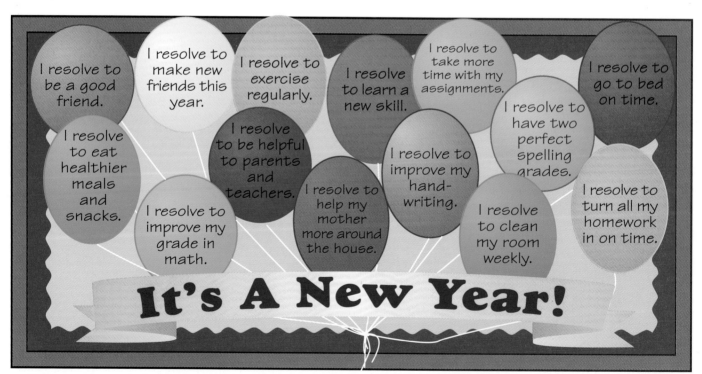

Encourage your students to set self-improvement goals. Talk privately with each student to determine an area in which he feels he could use some improvement. Have him choose a goal for the new year and write it on a balloon-shaped cutout. Display the balloons using yarn or ribbon for string.

Marilyn Borden—Gr. 3, Castleton Elementary School, Bomoseen, VT

Set the mood for wintertime reading with this motivational display. Duplicate several copies of the mitten pattern (page 80) onto sheets of pastel construction paper. Students complete, cut out, and display a mitten shape for each book they read. Create near-blizzard conditions by scattering snowflake cutouts around the board!

Carol Kenney and Lois Jones—Gr. 3, Scenic Hills School, Springfield, PA

This cherry tree is loaded with facts about our first president! Compile a fact list (*George Washington's Breakfast,* by Jean Fritz, is an excellent resource); then have each student record one fact onto a small circle cutout. Glue facts atop slightly larger circles cut from red construction paper, and attach construction-paper leaves and stems. Mount cherries on a tree cutout as shown. (See page 81 for George Washington pattern.)

Carol Kenney and Lois Jones—Scenic Hills School, Springfield, PA

Salute our country's past and future greats! Using the patterns on page 82, enlarge and cut out silhouettes of Lincoln and Washington. With the help of an adult volunteer, have each student create a silhouette cutout of himself. Mount the title and silhouettes as shown. Discuss the achievements of our country's past greats, then invite students to share their future aspirations. Now that's impressive!

Jean Hawkinson—Gr. 3, Mosel-Lakeview School, Howards Grove, WI

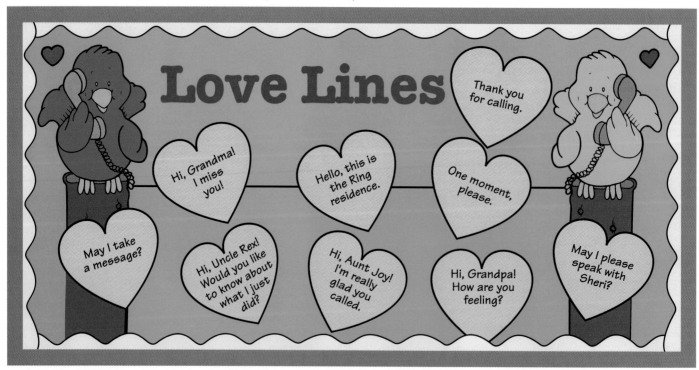

Ring in a collection of heartfelt messages as you promote well-mannered telephone conversations. Follow up a lesson about proper phone etiquette by having each youngster write a well-mannered telephone phrase on a construc-tion-paper heart. Mount the cutouts and characters (patterns on page 83 and 84) as shown. For added appeal, use coiled pipe cleaners for the telephone cords and a length of yarn or cord for the telephone wire. "May I ask who is calling?"

Diane Fortunato—Gr. 2, Carteret School, Bloomfield, NJ

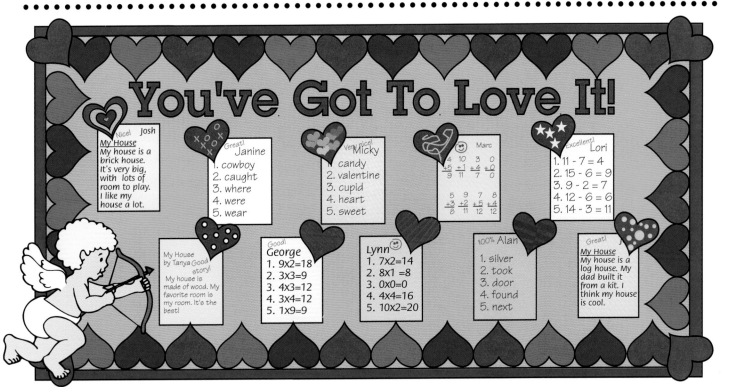

Showcase a hearty assortment of outstanding work with this seasonal display. Enlist the help of your youngsters in creating the colorful heart border. Then have each student decorate and personalize a heart-shaped paper topper. After each student has chosen a sample of her best work, display the work samples, paper toppers, and title as shown. Periodically ask students to replace their displayed work with more current samples. (See cherub pattern on page 85.)

Donna L. Hall—Gr. 1, Fairview Elementary, Jennings, MO

Boost your youngsters' self-esteem with this heartwarming display. Mount the title and a tree similar to the one shown. Personalize a large heart cutout for each student and one for yourself; then randomly distribute the cutouts, making certain that no one receives his own. Next have everyone write a sentence on his cutout that describes something he especially likes about the person who is named. Attach the hearts to the tree. Repeat the activity as often as desired.

Eleanor Sardo—Gr. 3, Thornton School, San Antonio, TX

SPRING

Spring Bulletin Boards.............................

When blustery, kite-flying weather arrives, display your students' favorite work samples on this becoming bulletin board. Cut out a white butter-paper cloud, and attach it to blue background paper before drawing on a facial expression and breezy swirls. Staple a favorite paper of each student to the board atop a sheet of construction paper. Have students make construction-paper kites complete with yarn strings and fabric tails. Attach the kites to the board near their work samples.

Margi Galligan—Gr. 1–3, Hooper, NE

There's a gold mine of knowledge at this display! To make the rainbow, have youngsters trace their hands atop sheets of construction paper and cut out the resulting shapes. Mount a pot cutout at the end of the rainbow. Next have each student personalize a coin-shaped booklet and list what he has learned during the school year on his booklet pages. Mount the booklets, a desired number of leprechauns (patterns on pages 86 and 87), and the title as shown. Have you ever seen such a pot of gold?

adapted from an idea by Catherine Crow—Gr. 1, Myers Elementary, Gainesville, GA

Display a wealth of outstanding student work this holiday season without pulling any shenanigans! Label and mount a shamrock cutout for each student. Each week allow students to choose papers they wish to exhibit. 'Tis a wee bit of magical motivation! (See page 88 for leprechaun pattern.)

Julie Renkes, Hutchinson, MN

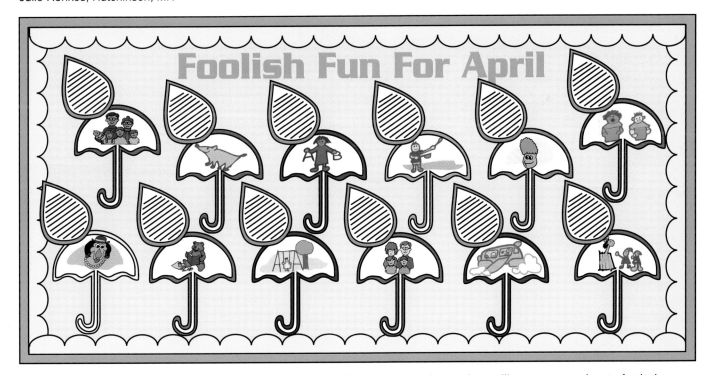

Make a splash with this seasonal activity and display. Have each student write a silly story on a sheet of raindrop-shaped writing paper. Then have him illustrate his story on drawing paper cut into the shape of an umbrella. (See patterns on page 89 and 90.) Mount each project atop colorful paper; then trim this paper to create an eye-catching border. Mount the completed projects and title as shown.

Vivian Campbell—Gr. 2, Knollwood School, Piscataway, NJ

Make a splash with this poetry-writing activity and display! Have each student write a poem about rain on a sheet of raindrop-shaped writing paper. Next have each student mount his project atop light blue paper, then trim the colored paper to create an eye-catching border. Mount the title, character, puddle, and raindrop projects as shown. It's the perfect project for a rainy day! (See patterns on pages 90 and 91.)

Diane Fortunato—Gr. 2, Carteret School, Bloomfield, NJ

Hooray for spring! Here's a festive display that's perfect for showing off springtime art projects! Have students twist brightly colored tissue-paper squares around their pencils and glue to a large umbrella shape cut from tagboard. Mount the completed umbrella cutout, along with a cart and pole cut from bulletin-board paper. Attach two paper-plate wheels with yarn spokes, and an assortment of student art (such as flowers and butterflies) to complete the display.

Debbie Grindrod
Parker, CO

Ease into spring with this eye-catching display. On background paper, sketch a pencil outline of a spring scene. Inconspicuously label a portion of the sketch for each student to color. When the coloring is completed, mount the breathtaking results! Happy spring!

Chava Shapiro, Beth Rochel Elementary, Monsey, NY

This hands-on display will make a splash! Mount three student-colored umbrella shapes as shown. Atop the shapes, display number cutouts representing multiplication products (or other math answers). Program raindrop cutouts (pattern on page 90) with corresponding problems. Program the back of each cutout for self-checking if desired; then punch a hole in the top of each and place the cutouts in a bucket. A student suspends the raindrops on pushpins above the corresponding umbrellas.

Mary K. Good, Seaford Christian Academy, Seaford, DE

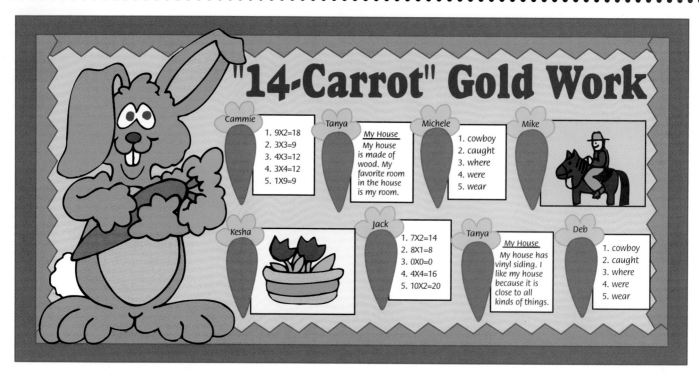

Exhibit a gold mine of impressive student work at this bunny bulletin board! Mount the character and title. Have each child create a personalized carrot cutout as shown. Then have each student choose a sample of her best work. Display each work sample with its corresponding carrot cutout. To keep the display current, encourage students to replace their work as frequently as desired. Hop to it! (See bunny pattern on page 92.)

Cover a spring bulletin board with a creative-writing assignment. Have each child write a paragraph titled "What Is Spring Fever?" Post finished paragraphs on the board with colorful, construction-paper flowers. After the display is up, discuss with children the meaning of "spring fever."

Annette Mathias, Partridge, KS

Take your youngsters' research skills to new heights! Mount ten balloon cutouts, ten yarn or curling-ribbon balloon strings, an assortment of cloud cutouts, and a title. Number and label each of ten cards with a question relating to a current study topic or theme. Attach one card atop each balloon. Also give each youngster a ten-page, balloon-shaped booklet. Challenge each student to research the questions, and then record the answer to each question on a different page of his booklet. Up, up, and away!

Laura Gayle McCord, Whitesburg Elementary, Carrollton, GA

A few seeds of encouragement will grow this colorful garden of accomplishments. In advance, have each youngster make three flowers using construction paper, wallpaper, gift wrap, or tissue paper. Then challenge each youngster to set three goals (such as memorizing multiplication facts through ten, earning a perfect score on a spelling test, and satisfactorily completing five homework assignments). When he achieves a goal, the child attaches one of his flowers to the display. (See patterns on page 93.)

Joan Steele, St. Louis, MO

A Crop Of Good Work

Since good work crops up everywhere, your students will enjoy making row markers for the "crops" in this garden. Select good work samples. Have each student glue his paper to a sheet of construction paper. Then have him glue on a vegetable or fruit picture cut from a magazine. After attaching a Popsicle® stick, have him display his work on the bulletin board. (See farmer pattern on page 94.)

Let's End The Year With A Bang!

End the year with a bang using a bear bearing balloons! For the last ten days of school, display a bear cutout (pattern on page 95) on a bulletin board with ten yarn lengths and ten inflated balloons. Each morning count the balloons and have your calendar helper pop one balloon using a large plastic knitting needle. (For safety, have the student close or cover his eyes while popping the balloon.) Have students count the balloons again. On the last day of school, lower the character as if he is falling and change the caption to read "See You Next Fall!"

Jeanne Thomas—Gr. K–1, Dugspur Elementary School, Dugspur, VA

There's no better time than the present to highlight the winning plays of the season. Using the pattern on page 96, mount the character and title as shown. Next have students illustrate their favorite memories of the school year on white construction-paper circles. Invite each of your little sluggers to share his completed project as you mount it on the display. Batter up!

Susan Pruitt, James Sales Elementary, Tacoma, WA

Set your sights on summer with this collection of picturesque postcards. Have each student draw and color a stamp in the top right-hand corner of a 5" x 8" index card. Next have each youngster illustrate one place he would like to visit during his summer vacation. Below his illustration, have him write a short postcard message as if he were really there. Before mounting the cards, use a colorful marker to write each child's vacation destination on his completed project. Bon voyage!

Terry B. Koopman—Gr. 1, Charles E. Bennett Elementary, Green Cove Springs, FL

Count down the final days of school at this end-of-the-year display. Have each student cut out and personalize a cloud shape. Mount the cutouts, the title, and a large kite shape with a lengthy tail. Determine the remaining number of school days; then label one cutout per day and attach the cutouts to the kite tail as shown. Each day have a different student remove one cutout from the tail. Build anticipation about next year by telling students something they have to look forward to each day.

Kathy Quinlan—Gr. 2, Charles E. Bennett Elementary, Green Cove Springs, FL

Take a sneak peek at your students' summer plans! Have each student cut out and decorate a pair of construction-paper shorts, then trim a sheet of writing paper to fit atop his cutout. After writing one or more sentences about his summer plans, have the student attach the paper to his cutout. Display the cutouts using clothespins and lengths of heavy string or plastic clothesline. Now that's a summer lineup!

Diane McMichael—Gr. K–4, Jefferson Elementary, Parkersburg, WV

Remember students having summer birthdays with this cheerful bulletin board. Enlarge the pattern on page 97, then color, cut out, and mount the clown face and bubble blower. Program construction-paper "bubbles" with student names and birthdates. Maybe summer birthdays aren't so bad after all!

Lois Benedict—Gr. 2, Lincoln Elementary School, White Bear Lake, MN

These busy bees are buzzing with accomplishments! Using the pattern on page 93, have students color and cut out bees. Tape pipe-cleaner antennae and yellow cellophane wings to the backs of the bees. (Add dimension to the wings by gathering the cellophane before taping.) Each student then writes one special accomplishment for the school year. Have students cut speech bubbles around their writing, then display the speech bubbles alongside their bees on the bulletin board.

Judy Peterson, Delta, UT

This student-made bulletin board acknowledges the fact that your students have met the "koala-fications" for being promoted to the next grade. Have each student make a koala by stapling a small paper plate to a larger one. Attach the plates so that the back of the small plate and the front of the larger plate are forward. For each student, duplicate two copies of the arm, leg, and eye patterns below on construction paper. Students cut out and glue the arms, legs, and eyes to the paper plates. Using the ear and nose patterns, supply each student with a fake fur nose cutout and two ear cutouts. About 1/4 yard of fake fur is sufficient for 20 koalas.

Vivian N. Campbell—Gr. 1, Grandview School, Piscataway, NJ

Patterns

For each student, duplicate two copies of the arm, leg, and eye patterns on construction paper.

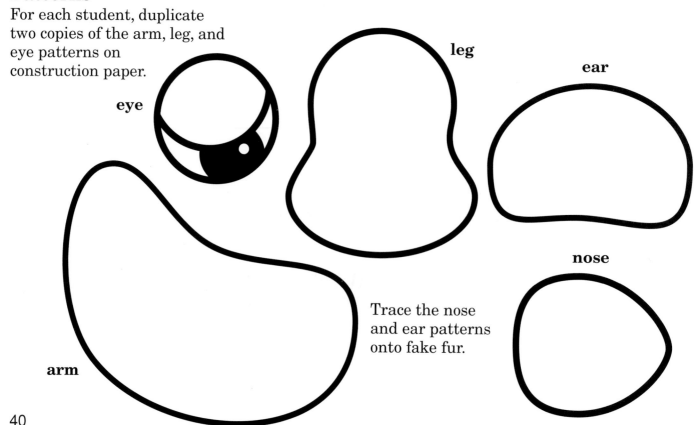

eye

leg

ear

nose

Trace the nose and ear patterns onto fake fur.

arm

ANYTIME

Anytime Bulletin Boards..........................

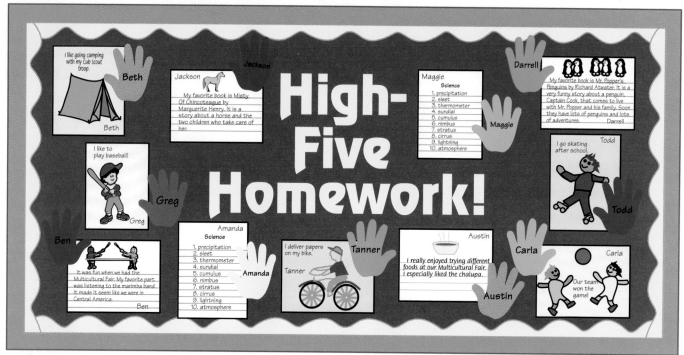

This hip display is sure to create enthusiasm for homework. Enlist the help of your youngsters in preparing a supply of high-five cutouts. To do this, have students trace their hands atop sheets of construction paper and cut out the resulting shapes. When a student's homework merits extra recognition, attach his paper to the display with a personalized high-five cutout. For added fun, give the youngster a high-five yourself!

Diane Fortunato—Gr. 2, Carteret School, Bloomfield, NJ

Students supply the cargo for this year-round express locomotive. Enlarge the engine pattern on page 108; then color, cut out, and mount. Attach boxcar and cargo shapes cut from bulletin-board paper as shown. After studying a part of speech, have each student cut five example words from newspapers or magazines to mount as cargo on the corresponding boxcar. Encourage students to utilize this "Parts Of Speech Express" when writing independently. All aboard!

Wendy Sondov—Gr. 3, St. Louis, MO

This eye-catching display may be just the bait to lure your youngsters into unlimited writing practice. Using the patterns on page 96, duplicate, laminate, and cut out a supply of colorful fish. Arrange the fish cutouts on a decorated bulletin board as shown. Using a wipe-off marker, label the fish with student-generated writing topics. Invite youngsters to visit the topic tank and hook up with writing topics at their leisure. When desired, wipe away the programming and brainstorm another fine catch of topics.

Melissa Miller—Gr. 1, Bart-Colerain Elementary, Christiana, PA

Here's a fun way to showcase your youngsters' accomplishments. Mount the title and a decorated clown cutout from page 98. (For a three-dimensional effect, attach a partially inflated red-balloon nose.) On construction-paper circles, have students write sentences describing their greatest achievements of the school year. Attach the programmed cutouts to the clown's bow tie. Isn't a round of applause in order for this outstanding performance?

Jana Jensen, Gillette, WY

With a few seeds of encouragement, youngsters can grow a colorful garden of literary accomplishments. Duplicate a supply of construction-paper flowers using the pattern on page 99. Each time a student reads a book, he completes the information on a duplicated flower. Then he uses markers or crayons to add desired details, cuts out the flower, and attaches it to the display. How nice! (See skunk pattern on page 100.)

adapted from an idea by Diana Curtis, Albuquerque, NM

Yee-haa! Old Mac's barnyard has animals just right for reinforcing short-vowel sounds. Using the patterns on pages 101 and 102, create and mount a display similar to the one shown. To introduce the display, choose one youngster to be Old Mac. As Old Mac points to each animal, lead the students in a chorus of "Old MacDonald Had A Farm." Instead of repeating the noise each animal makes, repeat the short-vowel sound in its name. Short-vowel sounds will be long remembered!

Marian DeGraffenreid—Gr. 2, Forsyth, MO

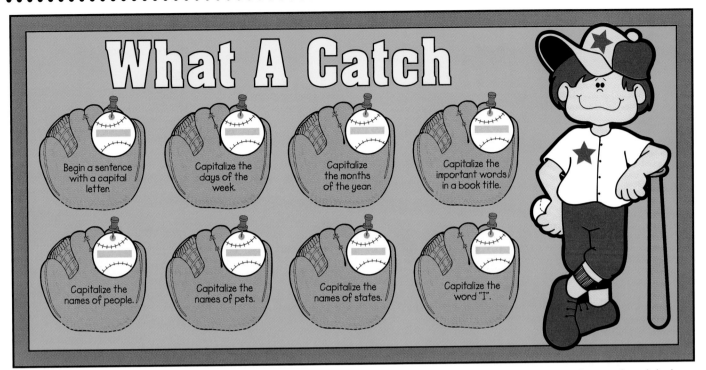

Use this manipulative display to reinforce a variety of capitalization rules. Duplicate and cut out gloves; then label each with a capitalization rule before mounting. Discuss and list examples for each rule. Have students write the examples on baseball cutouts. Punch holes in the cutouts for hanging; then store in a Ziploc® bag attached to the display. A student suspends each baseball cutout from the appropriately labeled glove on a provided pushpin. (See pages 103 and 104 for glove, baseball, and player patterns.)

Debbie Mackie, Granite Falls Elementary School, Granite Falls, NC

Showcase your students' special talents at this star-studded display. Have each student lend a hand fingerpainting a large circle cutout. When dry, mount the cutout and attach a paper strip decorated with glitter. Duplicate student copies of the star pattern (page 104) on construction paper. Have each student cut out, personalize, and illustrate a pattern. Encourage students to illustrate themselves doing activities that make them feel special. Everyone's a star!

Dianne Knight—Gr. 2, Frank C. Whiteley School, Hoffman Estates, IL

Inflate your students' interest in reading with this motivational bulletin board. Students complete and color one balloon book report (patterns on page 62) for each book they read. Encourage students to illustrate and attach book characters to their balloon baskets before mounting. Up, up, and away!

Carolyn Barwick, Madison Heights, MI

This eye-catching display helps students stay informed of notable news and upcoming events. Mount the steers (pattern on page 105), title, and speech balloons as shown. For easy management, laminate the speech balloons prior to mounting. Then, using a wipe-off marker, label the speech balloons with noteworthy items. To keep the news current, simply wipe away the programming and reprogram the balloons as desired.

Kathleen Darby—Gr. 1, Community School, Cumberland, RI

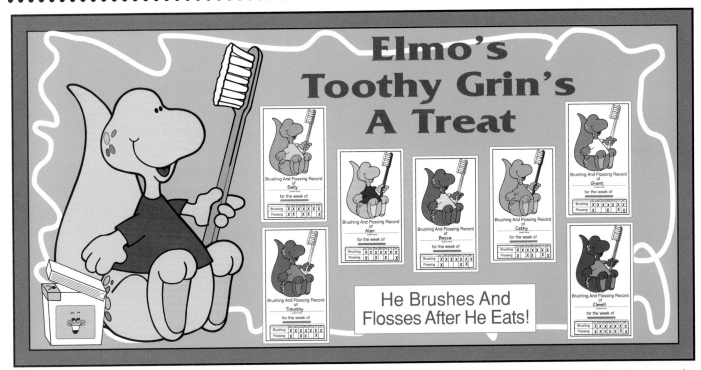

Smile! Elmo wants your students to have great dental hygiene. Enlarge Elmo from the brushing and flossing record on page 106. Color, laminate, and mount on the board. For a border of "toothpaste," pin a length of heavy yarn or cord to the board. Duplicate the brushing and flossing record on page 106 for each student. After recording their dental hygiene habits for one week, display these records along with Elmo.

Cackle, cackle, cluck, cluck. This hip chick creates quite a spectacle as her mound of eggs grows higher and higher. Introduce this incentive bulletin board with the hen sitting in the hay-filled box (pattern on page 107). Explain to your students that they will earn eggs for the hen's nest for each perfect test paper. Challenge the class to raise the chicken to the ceiling. When the hen reaches this monumental height, surprise your students with an "egg-ceptional" treat.

Charlotte Hall—Gr. 2
Lawrenceville, GA

Percival's Place-Value Express is chugging your way with a place-value display. To provide a place-value reminder and a practice area, enlarge, laminate, and mount the Place-Value Express (patterns on page 108) on a bulletin board. Place a wipe-off marker, a cloth, and several number cards nearby. Students may select a card, write the numbers on the correct positions on the train, and wipe them off. For older students, a decimal car may be added.

Kenneth T. Helms—Gr. 3, Irving Park Elementary, Greensboro, NC

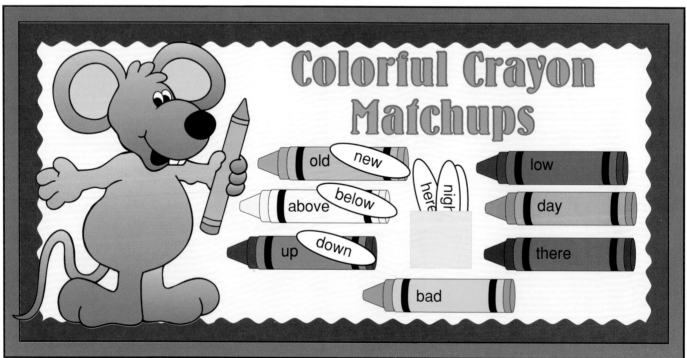

Duplicate a crayon pattern on various colors of construction paper to create this colorful matching activity. Laminate and program individual crayons and ovals (using permanent markers) with antonyms, synonyms, homonyms, math problems/solutions, or number words/numerals. Attach magnetic tape to the back of each oval. Mount character (pattern on page 109) and crayon cutouts. Insert a metal tack in each crayon cutout. Students remove the ovals from a library card pocket and match them to the corresponding crayons. Provide an answer key for checking.

Fran Petersen—Gr. 1–2, Ohio School, North Tonawanda, NY

Students will warm up to telling time with this eye-level bulletin board. Cut out orange circles and use clock faces (pattern on page 110). Paste the orange circles on yellow rays cut from poster board. Laminate the suns and mount on the bulletin board with times. Students use a wipe-off marker to draw hands to show the correct times. Change the times frequently.

Robert Kinker—Gr. 3, Bexley, OH

Students distinguish between telling, exclaiming, asking, and commanding sentences at this activity bulletin board. Mount and label birds with pockets for sorting as shown. Write sentences on cards and store in a pocket attached to the mailbox. Program cards for self-checking. Students sort cards to the appropriate birds.

Lisa Waters—Gr. 2, Our Mother of Sorrows, Yeadon, PA

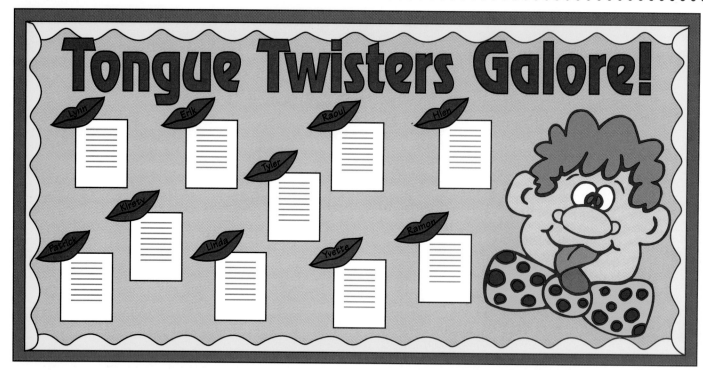

You'll create miles of writing motivation with this unique display. Mount the title and character; then have each youngster write a collection of tongue twisters. After the twisters have been edited and recopied, attach them to the display. For added fun, staple a pair of personalized lip cutouts to each child's paper. Invite students to update their tongue-twister collections as often as desired.

Kristin Goss—Gr. 3, Weigelstown Elementary, Manchester, PA

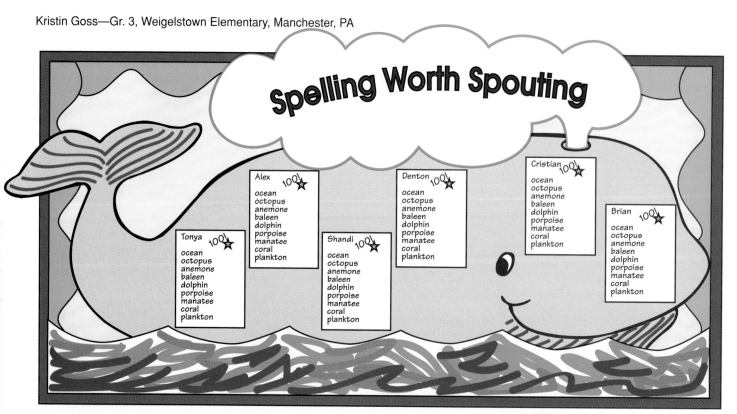

Showcase the spelling achievements of your youngsters in a big way! Enlist the students' help in painting and adding details to a large whale cutout. Mount the whale, a water spout, and the title as shown. If desired, have students use various shades of blue paint to finger-paint a length of paper; then trim one edge of the paper to create ocean waves. Mount the resulting project. Each week spotlight student papers that feature outstanding spelling.

Diane Fortunato—Gr. 2, Carteret School, Bloomfield, NJ

Provide extra motivation for fact memorization with this jungle scene. Mount palm branches, hibiscus flowers, and title. Hang a rope or string of ten knots for each student. Duplicate the monkey pattern on page 111 on brown construction paper. Students label, decorate, and glue monkeys to clothespins. Clip monkeys to ropes. When a student memorizes a set of facts, he may move his monkey to the next knot. Reward each student when his monkey reaches the top.

Jeani Z. Fullard—Gr. 3, Lealman Elementary, St. Petersburg, FL

Quack! Quack! Quack! These little ducklings are all lined up to reinforce number families and combinations. Using the pattern on page 55, duplicate, cut out, label, and display a family of ducks each time a new fact family is introduced. As new families are added, move existing families onto a classroom wall to free up space. In no time at all you'll have a progression of duckling families waddling around your classroom!

Barbara Hosek, Valencia, CA

Write Your Address

Encourage students to assist the mail carrier by addressing this giant envelope. Provide a large, laminated envelope as shown. For each student, duplicate the house pattern (page 112) and label with his address. Complete the bulletin board with a Ziploc® bag containing a cloth and a wipe-off marker. For practice, students take turns locating their addresses and copying them on the large envelope.

Jennifer B. Gardner—Gr. 2, Hillsville, VA

Hook your students on reading before it's too late! To make a worm, use a suitable material to loosely stuff a sock. Secure the stuffing by stitching or pinning closed the sock opening. Attach two wiggle eyes. Drape the worm over a length of clothes hanger that has been bent into a hook shape. Display the hook, worm, and title as shown. When a student completes a book, he creates a personalized fish cutout. Before displaying the fish, he labels it with the title of the book he read.

Motivate students to read, read, read at this one-of-a-kind library! To make each bookshelf, position and attach a strip of black bulletin-board paper as shown. Near the display keep a supply of colorful construction-paper strips in a variety of widths and lengths. After reading a book, a youngster writes his name and the title of the book he read on a strip. He then mounts the strip on the display. Read on!

Vallery McLaughlin, Charles Haskell Elementary, Edmond, OK

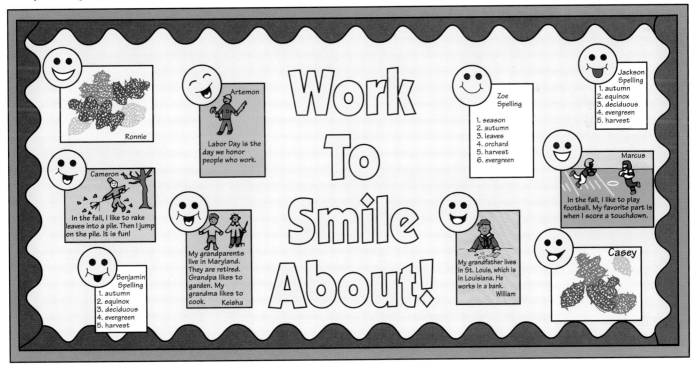

Create miles of smiles with this upbeat display! Enlist the help of your youngsters in preparing a supply of colorful happy-face cutouts. When a student's work makes you feel especially happy, write a cheerful comment on her paper and then attach her work to the display with a happy-face cutout. For added fun, also attach a happy-face sticker to the student's clothing. Now that's something to smile about!

adapted from an idea by Diane Afferton—Gr. 3, Chapin School, Princeton, NJ

Propel your students' writing enthusiasm to extraordinary heights with this year-round display. Laminate two rocket cutouts; then mount the rockets, the title, and a moon and several star cutouts as shown. Program each rocket with a type of written work; then invite youngsters to submit corresponding writing samples for the display. Mount students' edited writing atop the star cutouts. Reprogram the rockets each month and keep your students practicing a variety of writing skills.

Amy Turpin—Gr. 2, Murrayville-Woodson Elementary, Murrayville, IL

Who knows? Your youngsters' career goals may "egg-ceed" your greatest "eggs-pectations"! Using a variety of arts-and-craft materials, have students decorate large egg-shaped cutouts to illustrate their future career goals. Mount the resulting projects and title for all to enjoy.

Chantelle Lockwood, Urbana, OH

Use with "Quack, Quack, Welcome Back!" on page 6 and "Families Of 'Quacks'" on page 51.

Pattern

Use with "Things Go Better With Team-work!" on page 6 and "Help Wanted" on page 10.

Pattern

Use with " 'Bear-y' Special Students" on page 8.

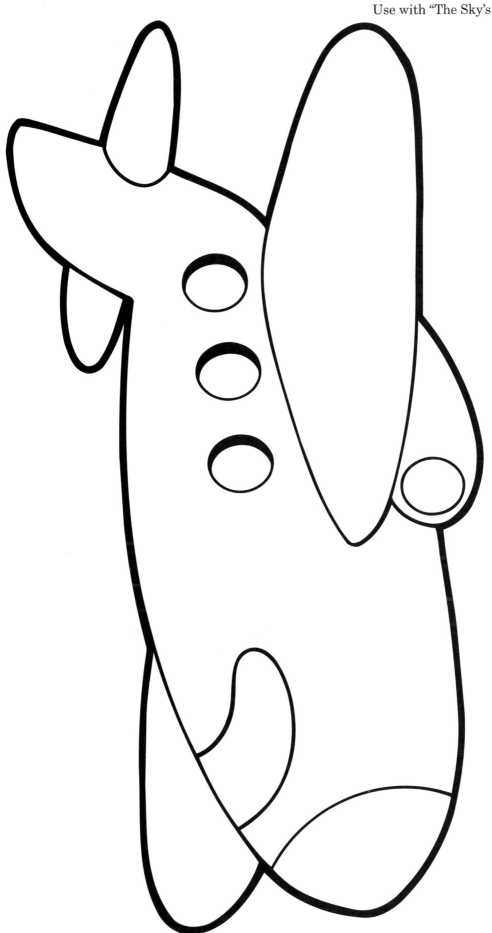

Patterns

Use balloon pattern with "Lifting Off To A Good Year!" on page 11.

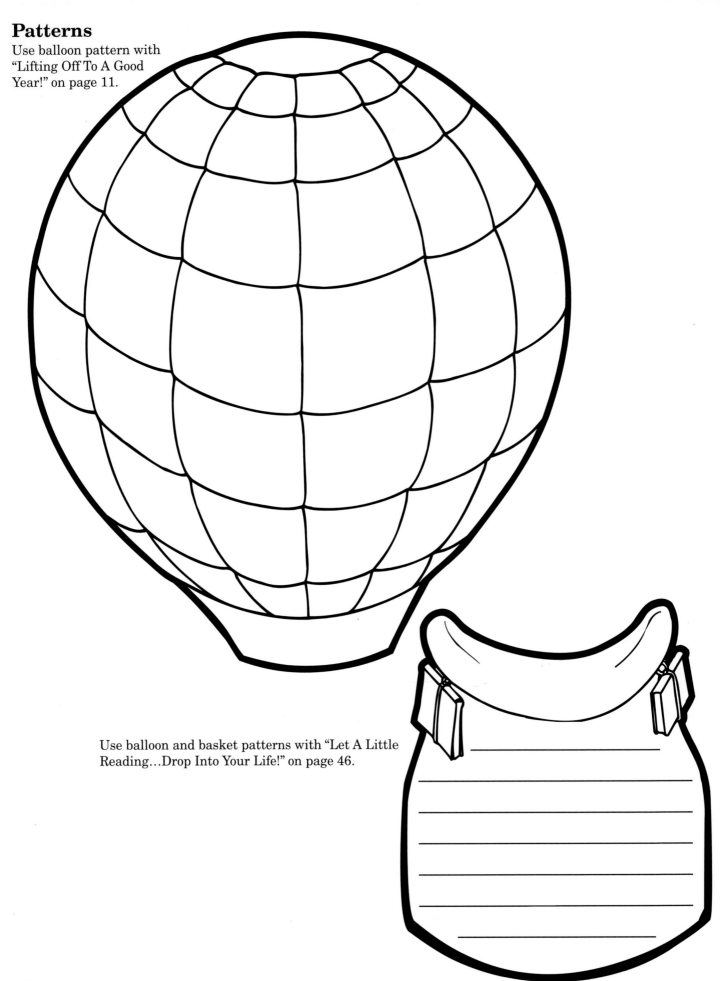

Use balloon and basket patterns with "Let A Little Reading…Drop Into Your Life!" on page 46.

62   ©1996 The Education Center, Inc. • *The Best Of* The Mailbox® *Bulletin Boards Primary* • TEC1451

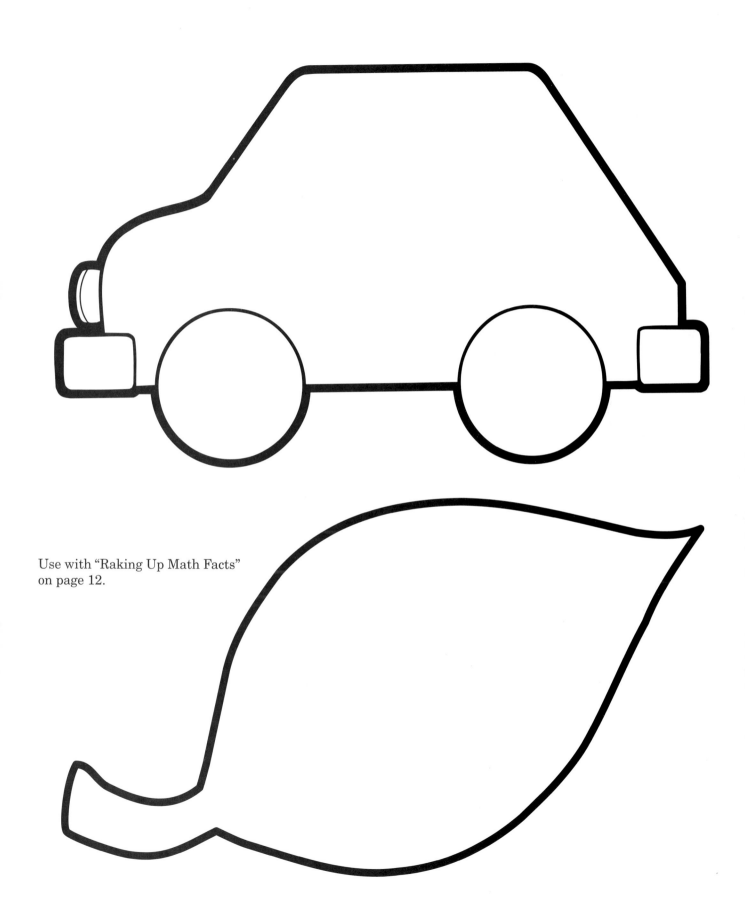

Use with "Raking Up Math Facts" on page 12.

Pattern

Use with "Sail On, Columbus" on page 13.

Finished ship

Steps:
1. Color and cut out the ship.
2. Cut three sails from light brown paper.
3. Draw and color a design on each sail.
4. Glue each sail to one end of a craft stick.
5. Glue the other end of each stick to the back of your ship.
   Now you are ready to set sail!

Use with "Sail On, Columbus" on page 13.

Sail On!

After seven years of petitioning, Columbus finally convinced King Ferdinand and Queen Isabella of Spain to finance his westward journey. His ships—the Niña, the Santa María, and the Pinta—were from 74 to 82 feet long. The sails were brownish because they were woven of flax. All of the sails were decorated with crosses and symbols.

Let children hit the high seas on these seaworthy ships! For each child, duplicate the pattern on page 64 on white construction paper. Before students begin, explain that the parts of the ships above the water-line were usually painted bright colors. After students have colored and cut out their ships, give each child three craft sticks and a 3" x 9" strip of brown paper bag. Have each student cut his paper strip into three sails, then decorate the sails using crayons or markers. To complete his ship, have each youngster glue a sail to one end of each craft stick, then glue the opposite ends of the sticks to the back of his ship cutout.

One Man's Big Dream

Columbus was a man possessed by the dream of discovering a shorter route to the Indies and its treasures. His dream was so important to him that he spent years petitioning Europe's rulers for help.

Ask your students about their biggest dreams. Find out what incredible feats they would like to have others remember as their accomplishments. Then on a piece of paper, have each student copy and complete the sentence starter "My big dream is to _____." Edit the sentences for spelling; then have each child copy and personalize his final work on a white construction-paper cloud cutout. If desired, have each student add a border of silver glitter to his cutout. Invite each youngster to share his big dream as you mount his cutout on the display titled "Sail On, Columbus."

Patterns

Use with "The Great Pumpkin Thinks That Great Work Is A Treat!" on page 14.

Pattern

Use with "Harvest Of Good Work" on page 14.

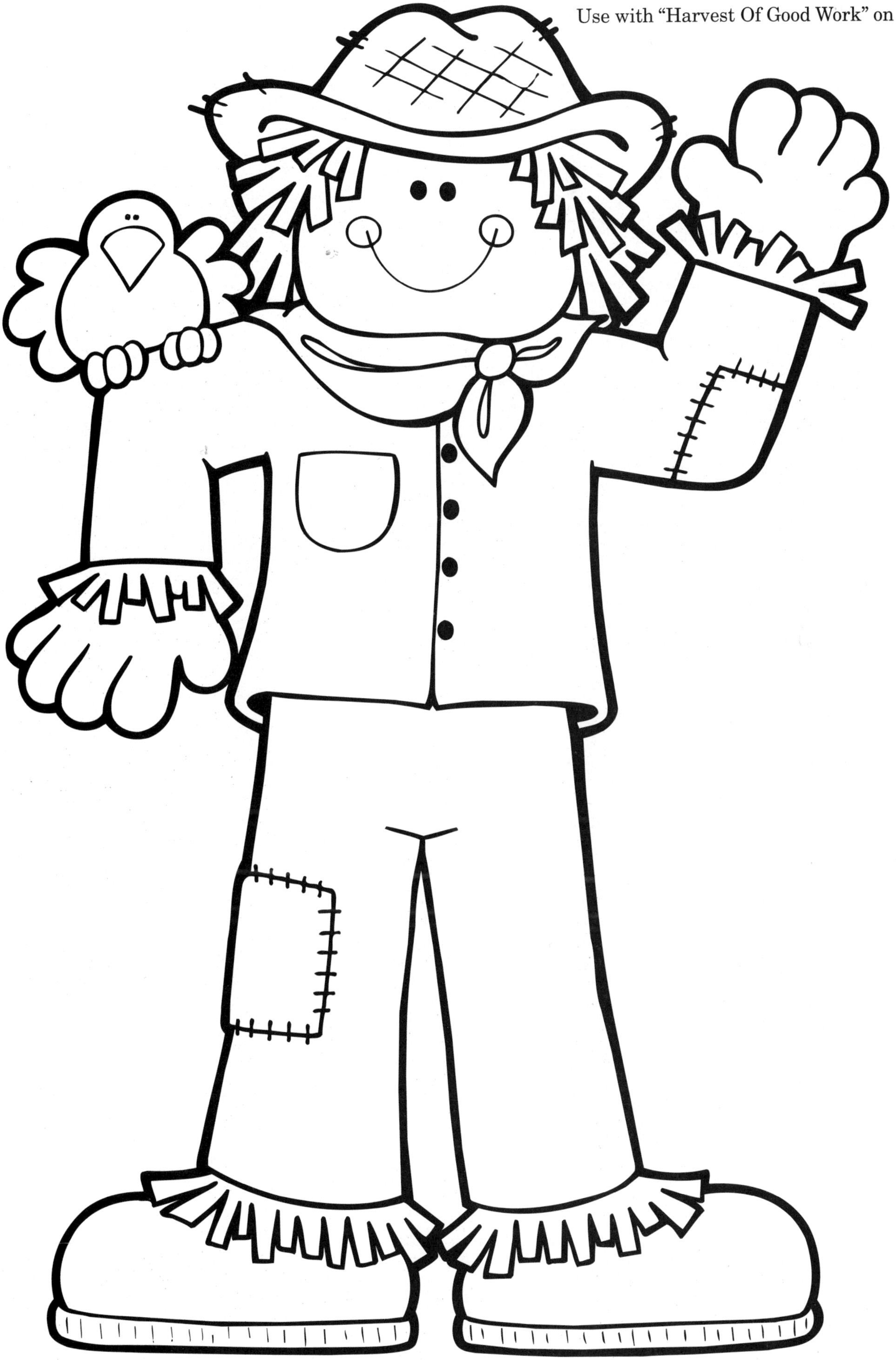

Pattern

Use with "We Will Ha-ha-haunt You!"
on page 15.

Riddle answers:
 1. booties
 2. Lazybones
 3. a spelling bee
 4. "Ghoul-lashes"
 5. a "neck-tarine"

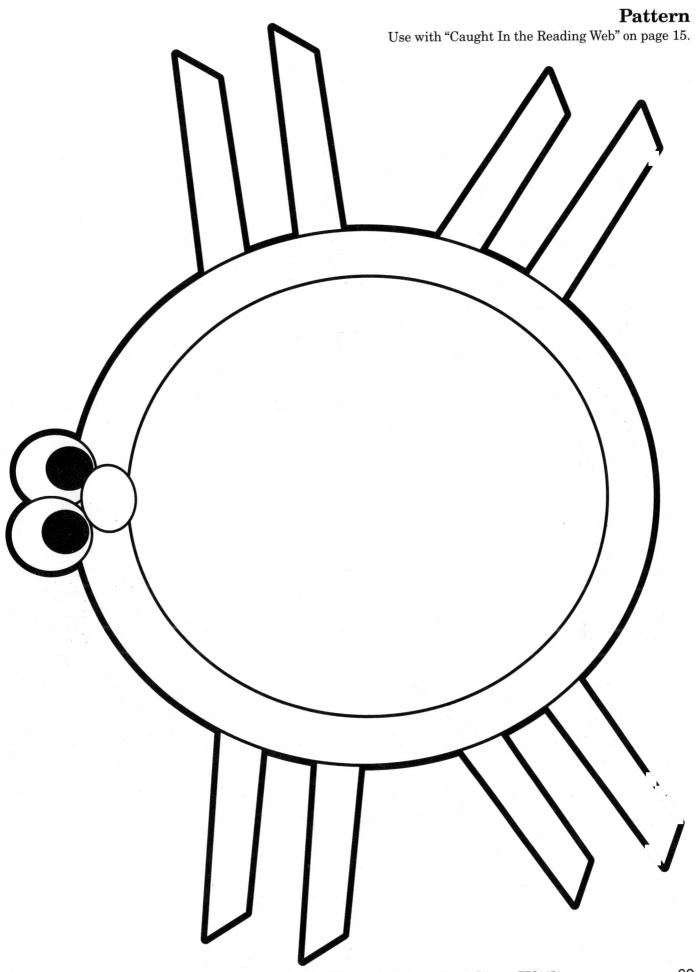

Pattern
Use with "We're Nuts About Our Work!" on page 16.

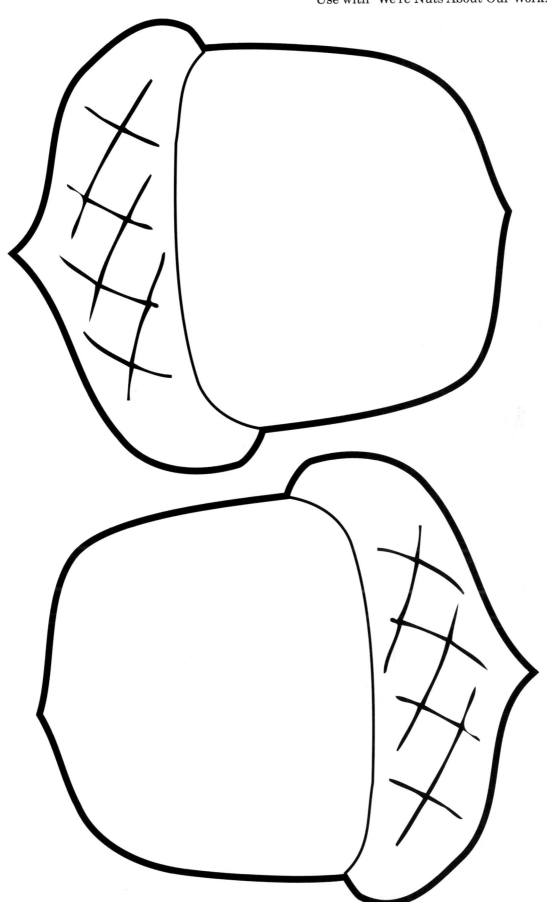

Patterns
Use turkey body with "We're In Step With Thanksgiving!" on page 17.
Use turkey body and feathers with "Gracias Por..." on page 18.

Pattern

Use with "Stir Up A Thankful Thanksgiving!" on page 16.

Recipe For A Thankful Thanksgiving

Ingredients:

Instructions:

Patterns

Use with "A Harvest Of Thanks!" on page 17.

Patterns

Use leaves with
" 'Tree-mendously'
Thankful Thoughts!" on
page 18.

Pattern

Have each student decorate Frosty's old silk hat with holiday designs. Create a hat-shaped tagboard cutout using the pattern below. Trace the shape onto black paper and cut out. Using construction-paper scraps, sequins, and miscellaneous craft supplies, decorate Frosty's hat with an original design. Glue on generous glitter outlines for a magical touch. Display these hats using the bulletin-board suggestion on page 22. "Thumpity, thump, thump. Thumpity, thump, thump. Look at Frosty go. Thumpity, thump, thump. Thumpity, thump, thump. Over the hills of snow!"

Pattern

Use with "Warm Up To Books!" on page 25.

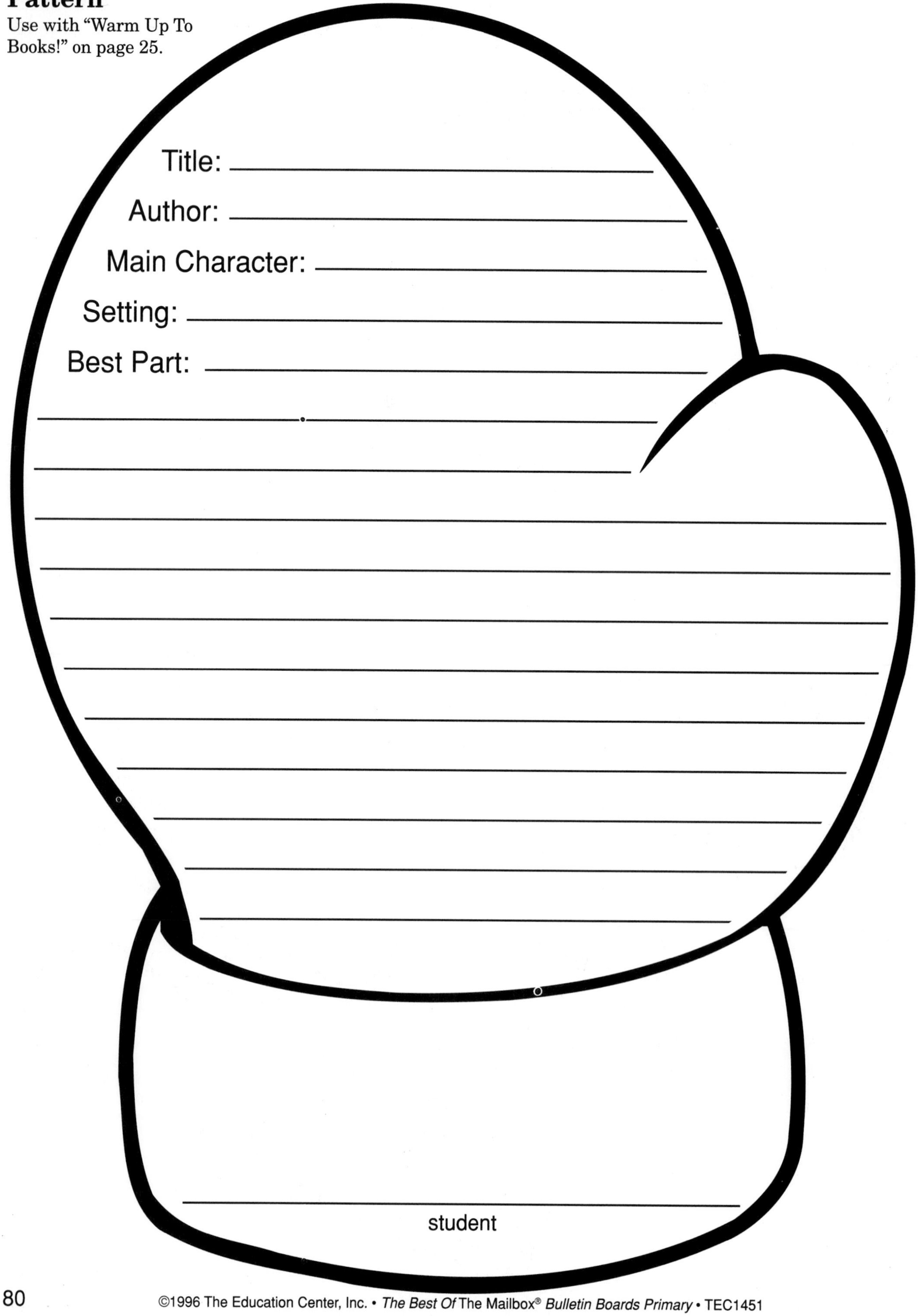
Title:
Author:
Main Character:
Setting:
Best Part:
student

Patterns

Use with "Past Greats And Future Greats!" on page 26.

Pattern

Use with "Love Lines" on page 26.

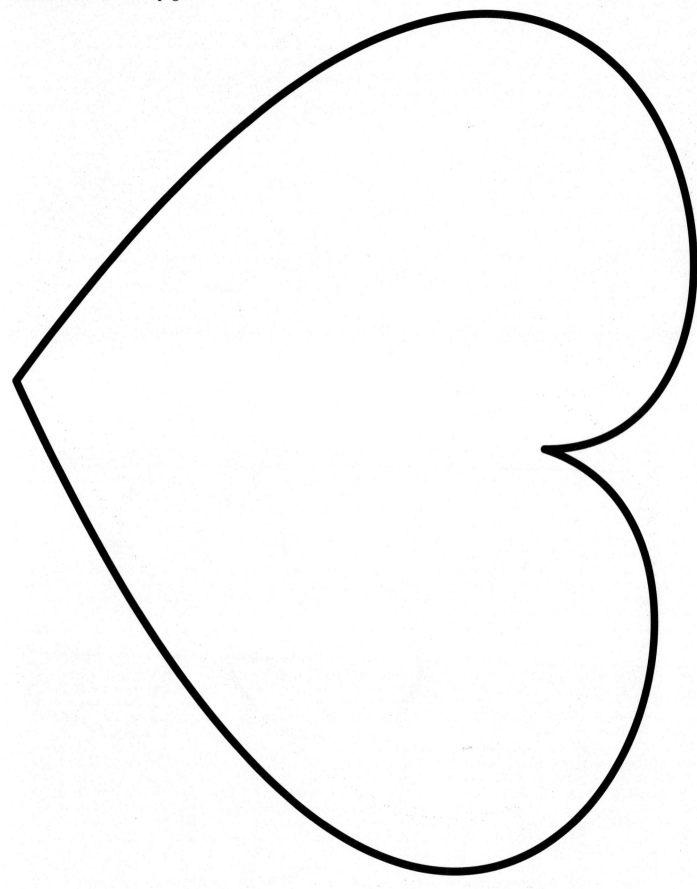

Patterns

Enlarge leprechaun patterns to use with "We've Struck It Rich..." on page 30.

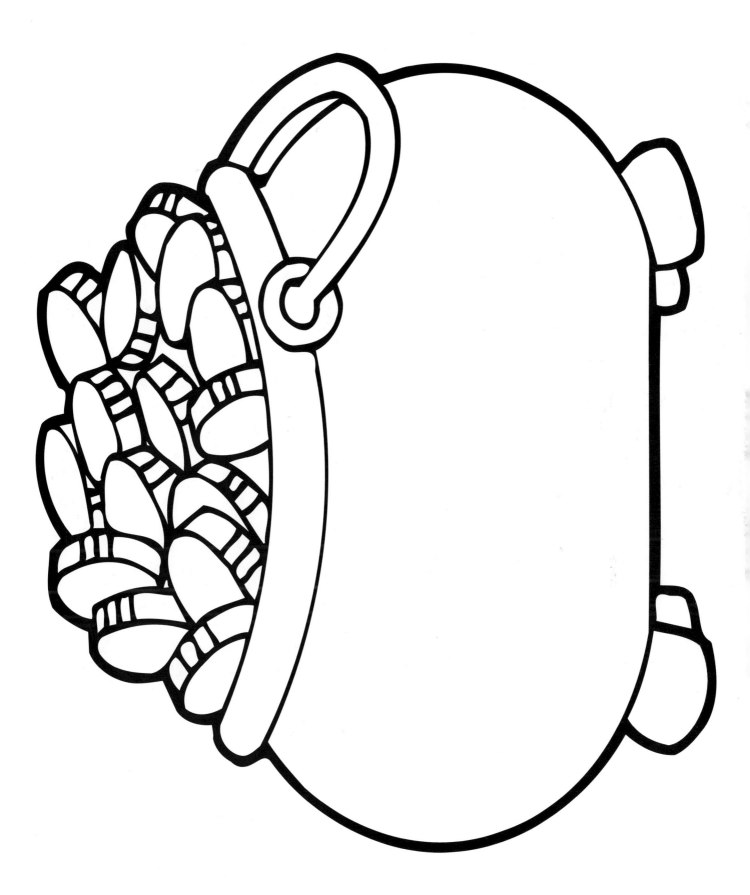

Pattern

Enlarge leprechaun pattern to use with "These Kids Are..." on page 31.

Pattern

Use with "Foolish Fun For April" on page 31, "Splish-Splash Poetry" on page 32, and "Dropping In On Math!" on page 33.

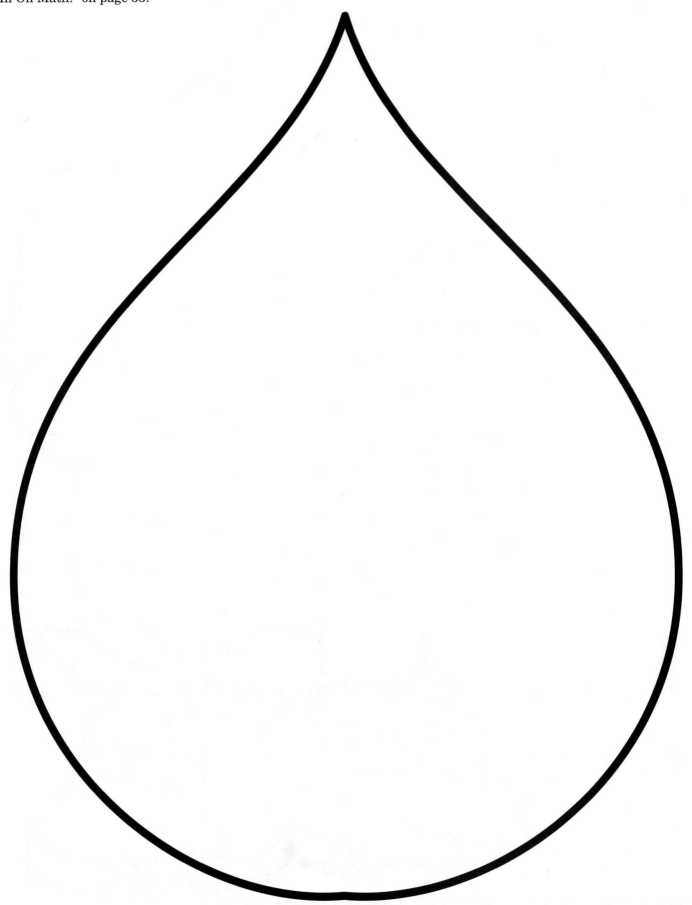

Pattern
Use with " '14-Carrot' Gold Work" on page 34.

Use with "We've Been Busy Bees!" on page 39.

Pattern
Use with "A Crop Of Good Work" on page 36.

Patterns

Use fish with "Topic Tank" on page 43.
Use baseball player with "We've Had A Ball..." on page 37.

Pattern

Use with "No Funny Business This Year!" on page 43.

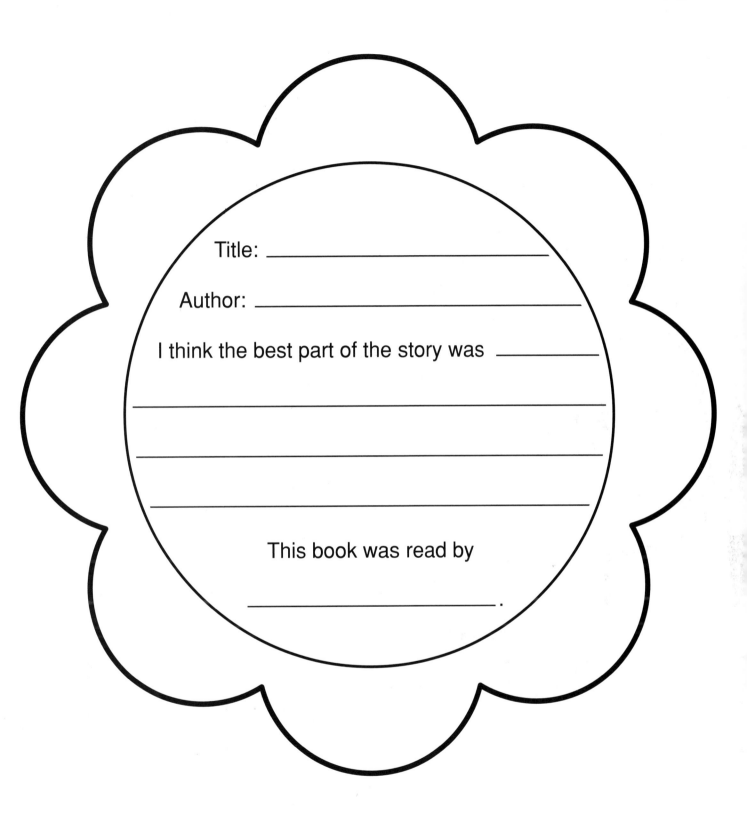

Title: _____

Author: _____

I think the best part of the story was _____

_____

_____

_____

This book was read by

_____ .

Pattern

Use with "Bloomin' Good Books!" on page 44.

Patterns

Use with "Old MacDonald Had A Farm!" on page 44.

MacDonald's
Short-Vowel Farm

Old
Mac

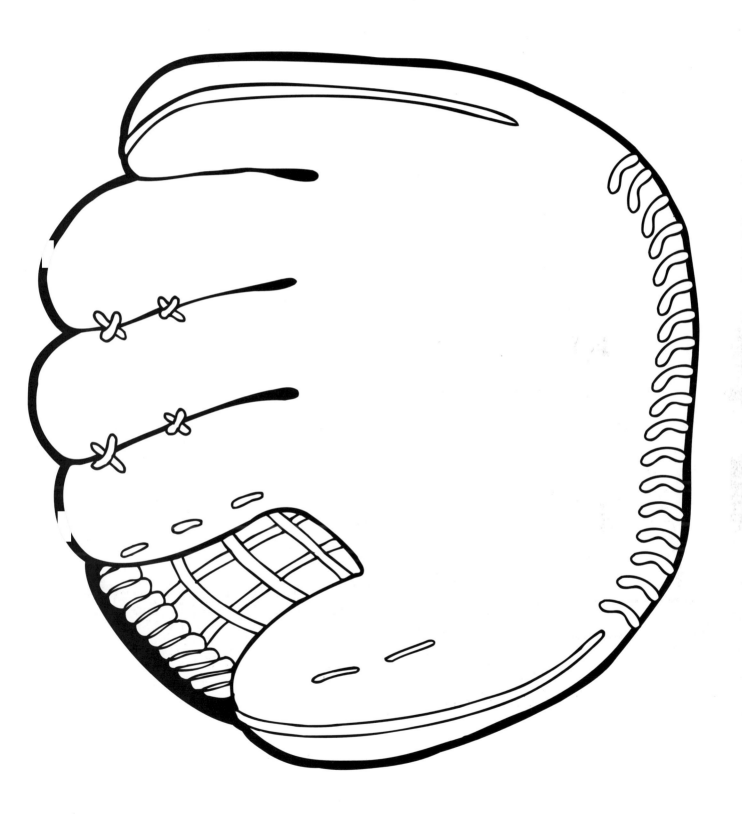

Patterns

Use with "What A Catch" on page 45.

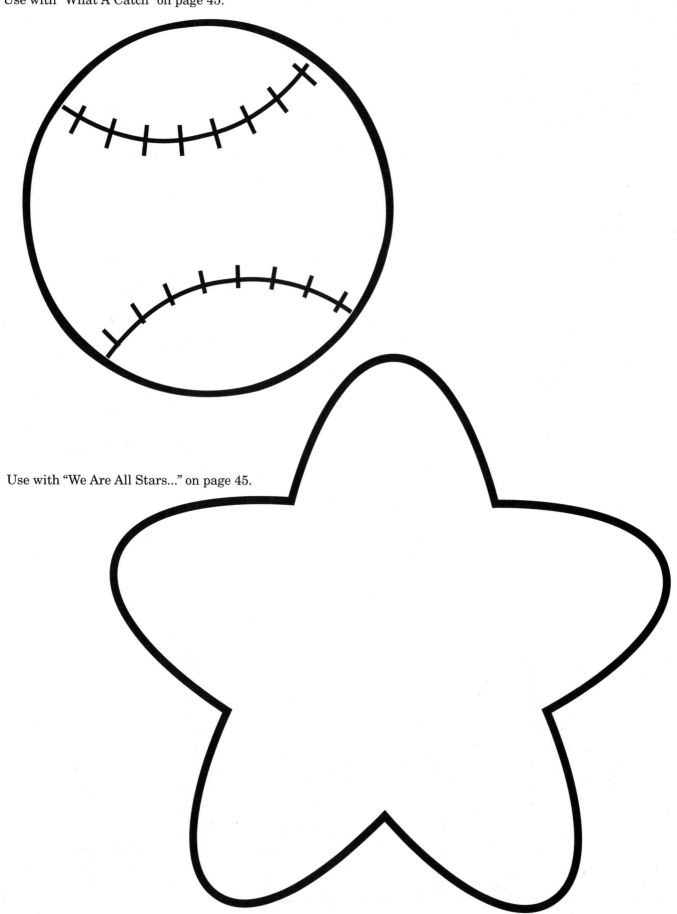

Use with "We Are All Stars..." on page 45.

Pattern

Use with "Elmo's Toothy Grins..." on page 47.

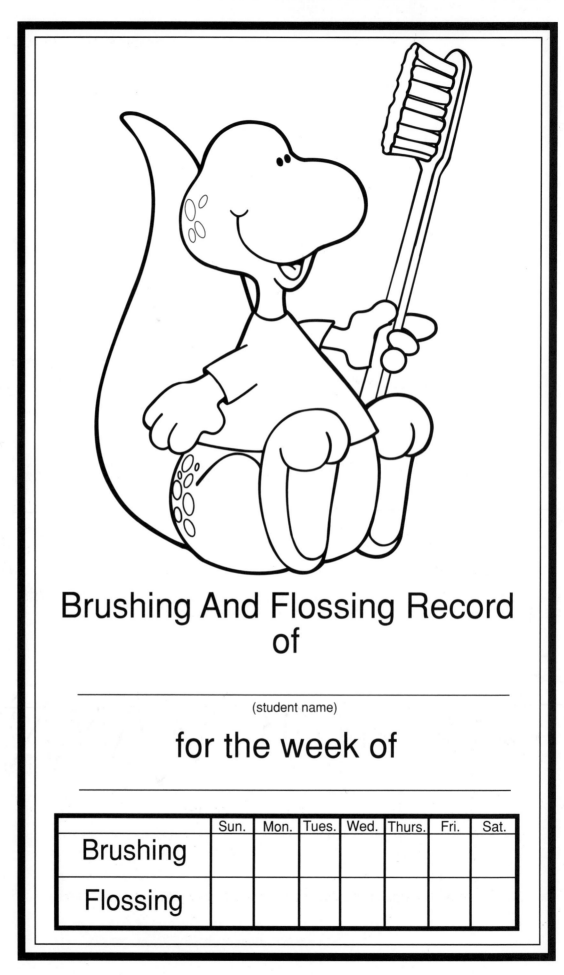

Brushing And Flossing Record
of

_____

(student name)

for the week of

_____

	Sun.	Mon.	Tues.	Wed.	Thurs.	Fri.	Sat.
Brushing							
Flossing							

Patterns

Use with "Place-Value Express" on page 48 and "Parts Of Speech Express" on page 42.

Pattern
Use with "Warm-Up Time" on page 49.

Pattern
Use with "Write Your
Address" on page 52.

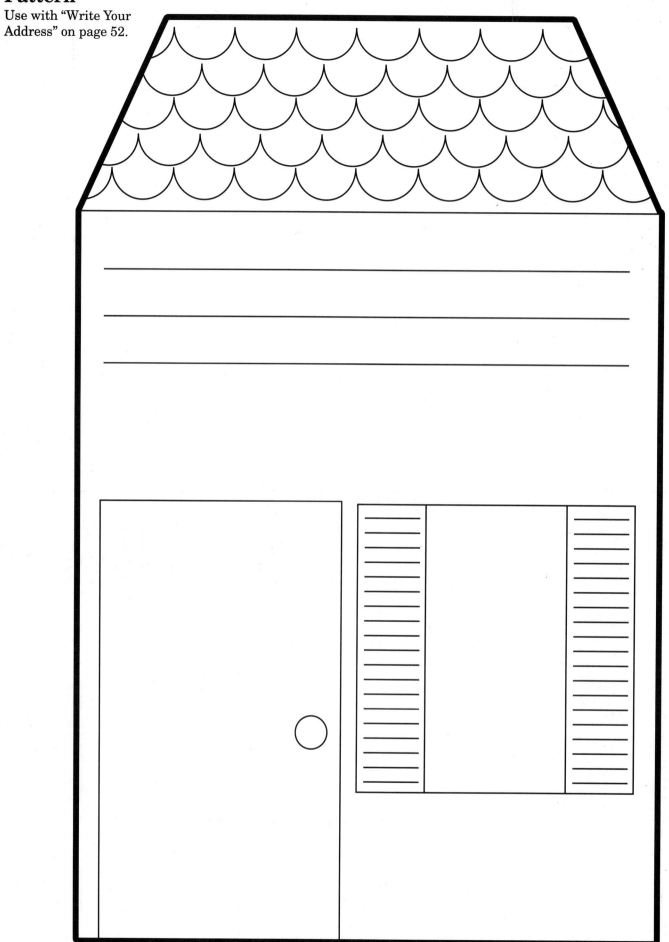